A message to parents from

Johnson's®

The most precious gift in the world is a new baby. To your little one, you are the centre of the universe. And by following your most basic instincts to touch, hold and talk to your baby, you provide the best start to a happy, healthy life.

Our baby products encourage parents to care for and nurture their children through the importance of touch, developing a deep, loving bond that transcends all others.

Parenting is not an exact science, nor is it a one-size-fits-all formula. For more than a hundred years Johnson & Johnson has supported the healthcare needs of parents and healthcare professionals, and we understand that all parents feel more confident in their role when they have information they can trust.

That is why we offer this book as our commitment to you to provide scientifically sound, professionally reviewed guidance on the important topics of pregnancy, babycare and child development.

As you read through this book, the most important thing to remember is this: you know your baby better than anyone else. By watching, listening and having confidence in your natural ability, you will know how to use the information you have in your hands, for the benefit of the baby in your arms.

Contents

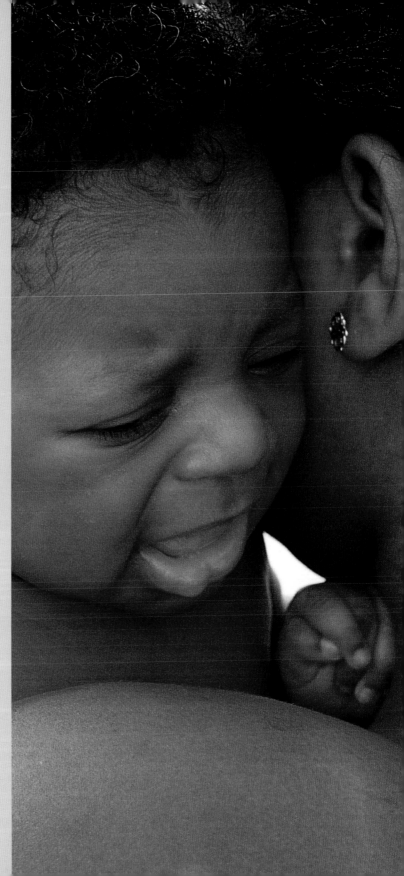

" I can feel my heartbeat quickening when I hear Alexa crying. It really does **trigger** a strong reaction. I need to respond to her and find ways of **calming her down.**"

GINA is mum to nine-month-old Alexa

1

Why do babies cry?

Imagine for a moment what life might be like if your baby never cried. You would have no way of knowing that he was hungry, ill or in pain, or simply needed a hug. Crying is an important part of your baby's survival mechanism. It's a signal that is virtually impossible for parents to ignore, and a highly effective way of ensuring that you will quickly respond to his needs, whatever they happen to be.

The significance of crying

Your baby's cry is designed to grab your attention. On hearing it, your body produces stress hormones that increase your blood pressure and heart rate and tense your muscles. You are very keen to solve the crying.

Crying also promotes "attachment" – the way in which you bond with your baby when love grows between you. It does this by ensuring that you keep your baby close to you and provide him with plenty of loving attention. Indeed, research has found that babies who have formed a poor emotional attachment to their parents may sometimes cry inconsolably to get the attention they desperately need.

To begin with, crying is also your baby's main "language" for expressing his needs. Then, as other ways of communicating (especially speech) develop, you will notice that your baby cries less because he doesn't need to rely on crying as a way of making himself understood. Having said that, he will continue to cry throughout childhood, and adulthood, to signal distress.

Patterns and peaks

Your baby cries most during the first three months, after which the rate of crying tends to drop to about half its earlier level. Some babies naturally cry more than others, and there is evidence that these *relative* amounts of crying remain up to one year of age. This means that babies who cry more than others in the first three months are likely to still be crying more until the age of one, even though they are crying less than they were. Perhaps surprisingly, your baby's level of

How long do babies cry?

Most Western babies cry on average for approximately:

- two hours a day in the first three months
- one hour a day in the four-to-12-months period.

Remember, these are *average* figures. Many babies do cry more than this, so don't worry if yours seems to be one of them. Interestingly, studies of non-Western communities where there is more frequent body contact and demand feeding suggest that babies there seem to cry less.

Questions & Answers

My three-month-old baby can be very happy, gurgling at her mobile or listening to music one minute, then quite suddenly she starts screaming and goes into a meltdown. Why is this?
It is likely that your baby is showing you that she has become over-stimulated. When this happens, move her to a more peaceful area away from too many toys, sights and sounds. You can try to spot this coming from her body language – she may turn her head away or squeeze her eyes shut, for example, before the crying frenzy starts.

crying is not at its highest when he is a newborn. The rate of crying gradually increases from birth until a baby is around six weeks old, then it subsides. This is often referred to as the developmental crying peak.

In the first three months, evening crying makes up about 40 per cent of the daily total, and about half of all parents report an evening crying peak – usually early evening (see pages 30–35).

Between the ages of about nine and 12 months, night-time crying

becomes more common, although again this is often a pattern shown by babies who have been excessive criers up until then (see page 9).

Coping with change

There is considerable recent evidence to show that a lot of what causes your baby to cry during the first few months is simply developmental. From birth, your baby has to go

THE FIRST CRY
Your baby's first cry announces that he is taking his first breaths, and is missing the security of the womb.

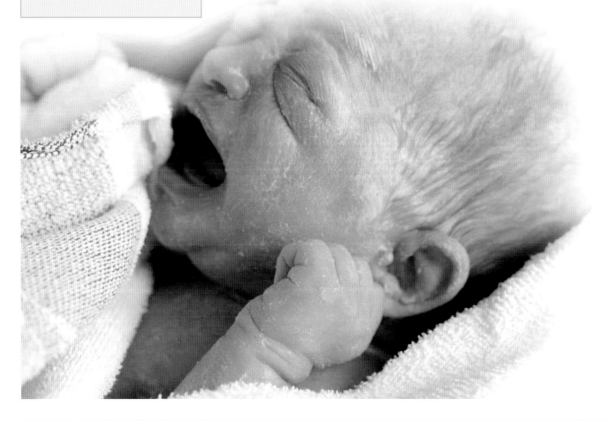

Sensitive babies

Some babies can be shown to have a low sensory threshold – in other words they are more sensitive than other babies. They seem to miss the safety of the womb and are readily overwhelmed by new experiences. You can probably recognize this if your baby is one who dislikes being bathed or undressed. Typically, sensitive babies tend to:

● change more rapidly from one behaviour state to another, for example from sleeping to crying

● be easily startled more often

● more frequently tense or jerk their arms and legs.

Sensitive babies may cry as a result of food passing down through their digestive system, having wind, and even from the physical feelings of their own bodies, such as the movement of their arms and legs.

External sensations may be too much for these babies. Sounds, light, smells or faces suddenly coming too close to them, even being picked up and held, especially by a number of different people, can be upsetting.

If you recognize your baby as being of a sensitive nature, he will enjoy calm, peaceful surroundings and careful handling (see page 26).

Checklist

To help interpret your baby's needs, think of his crying as a graded signal, the level of which represents increasing distress.

● **Intensity** Consider how loud the crying is. Does the intensity decrease when you hold your baby?

● **Constancy** Note how long your baby's crying lasts. Does it stop when you hold him?

● **Pattern** Note also when the crying occurs. Is it mainly in the morning, afternoon, evening or night? Before, during or after feeds? Is it every day, or more on weekdays than at the weekend? Is it when he's missed a nap, after being handled a lot or being in a stimulating environment?

● **Length of crying** How many hours a day does your baby's crying last, on average?

through huge changes, physically, socially and psychologically. It's normal for a baby to have bouts of more persistent crying before a particular developmental stage. It may be connected to major changes in the baby's brain and nervous system when a new developmental challenge is met.

This means that all babies will cry a certain amount, no matter what you do to try to soothe them. So it is not always helpful to think that "something's wrong" or to wear yourself out trying to find solutions to stop the crying.

Excessive crying

Excessive crying is defined as more than three hours' crying in a 24-hour period. As many as one in four babies, from newborn to three months of age, display this level of crying. Many theories of why babies cry excessively have been tested by researchers but have proven to be unfounded. These include over-feeding or under-feeding, trapped wind, "colic" (see pages 30–35), the mother's age, the sex of the baby, allergies, the parents' IQ or educational level, whether they are first-time parents, spoiling, and even whether the baby's mother smoked or drank coffee in pregnancy.

Your baby's temperament

Some babies are more "challenging" than others, and it is simply in their temperament to cry more. It is worth considering that your baby may need a very high level of care and closeness for a while to aid his development, and that crying is a vital, if rather exaggerated, way to ensure he gets the necessary attention. Even if you have a challenging baby, remember that:

● your baby's crying is *never* his "fault"

● it's certainly not your fault, either

● it does not mean that your child will grow up to be difficult or bad-tempered.

There is no evidence that excessive crying has any effect on development or behaviour beyond the first year. He *will* grow out of this stage.

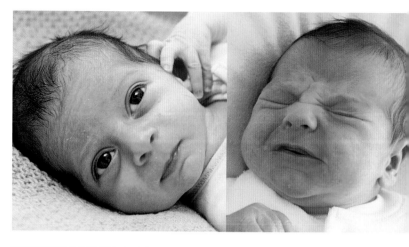

WHAT'S HIS TEMPERAMENT?
He may be active, sensitive, easily over-stimulated or a bit of everything. Getting to know him will help you comfort him.

Sensing your tension

It has been suggested that a baby can pick up on a parent's tension. You may find that even though you try your best to soothe your crying baby, someone else – your partner, health visitor or a friend – can calm him down more easily.

As a new mother, you may find this very disheartening. You may even start to think that your baby doesn't like you. It is only too easy to feel rejected when your baby seems to dislike being held, or thrashes around crying when you try to carry him in a sling.

While it is tempting to think that you must be doing something wrong, the likelihood is that you are feeling so upset by the crying because of your strong emotional bond with your baby, you become tense and irritable. Your baby senses this build-up of tension in you and cries all the more. So a vicious circle begins. Make the most of others' offers of help – and if they can soothe your baby in the process, so much the better!

What those cries could mean

Research may not support the theory that a baby's cries sound different depending on his needs, but many parents believe that they can identify several types of crying from their babies – for example, hunger, pain or irritability – and this helps them try to find ways to soothe them.

● **Hunger** In the early days, hunger is most likely to be the main reason for your baby's cries. It is the most obvious, and easiest to deal with. A hunger cry is very persistent and is unlikely to stop until your baby is fed.

● **The need for attention** A baby who needs your attention and probably wants a cuddle may sound "grizzly".

● **Pain or fright** If your baby is in pain or has been startled by something, his cries are likely to be a very sharp yell.

● **Illness** Although this is rarely the reason that he's crying, an ill baby's cry may be unusual in some way – more high-pitched, for example (see page 59).

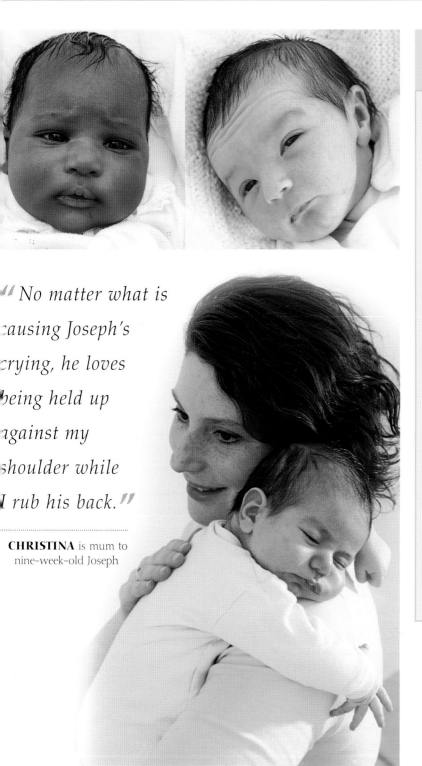

" No matter what is causing Joseph's crying, he loves being held up against my shoulder while I rub his back."

CHRISTINA is mum to nine-week-old Joseph

Questions & Answers

I had a long and difficult labour, and eventually a forceps delivery. My son is five weeks old now and seems hard to settle. Has his birth experience had anything to do with it?

It's true that some babies may cry more following a complicated delivery or obstetric interventions, such as a forceps, ventouse or Caesarean birth.

Also, babies who have been born prematurely, or who have spent time in special care, may cry more and need especially sensitive care. It could be that they are experiencing more discomfort or pain, or it may just be that they are finding it harder to cope with all the normal sights and sounds because of their immaturity.

Consider also the effect the birth may have had on you. A negative birth experience can lead to mothers taking less pleasure in their babies, who may then cry more. A baby who is difficult to console can in turn increase a mother's feelings of inadequacy, which makes the situation worse. Talk this through with your doctor, who can offer advice and check that your baby is well.

" Ali **cried a lot** during the first two months. We tried everything to comfort her, but there were times when nothing helped her. Happily, **she settled** at around 12 weeks. What a relief! "

DEBBIE is mum to six-month-old Ali

2

Crying in your newborn

Imagine how it feels for your baby to leave behind the warm, safe womb where, for the past nine months, she's been happily floating with all food and drink on tap. It is a shock for her to enter this strange, new world and there are many different experiences to cope with. No wonder babies cry soon after they are born!

Adjusting to the world

Newborn babies must make a big adjustment in the first few days of life outside the womb. Many cope with this by sleeping a great deal, firmly shutting out all sensations from the noisy, bright environment in which they have recently arrived.

But for some babies, the shock to their senses caused by this arrival is probably just too much, and they express their feelings of discomfort by crying vigorously due to the many unfamiliar sensations of light, noise and sometimes even the touch of many different people.

Learning from your baby

There is always a "learning time" with a new baby, even if she is not your first child. Your baby is an individual, so it is important for you both to get to know one another. In the early weeks, a lot of your baby's crying probably happens simply because you have not yet learned what your baby likes and dislikes. This takes time and paying attention to all your baby's verbal and behavioural communication cues.

Luckily, you have already had a headstart in getting to know her in the womb. From her movements, you may have known when she was asleep or awake, whether she was restless or had hiccups, and you may notice similarities after birth.

The emotional and physical connections between you have already been firmly established – so much so that she relies now on your voice and touch, even your heart rate and breathing, to help her settle into her new existence.

Spend quiet time observing your new baby. This helps you to get to know her and understand her needs. Try not to compare her with other babies, or with anything you may hear or read.

In tune with your baby

Until you tune into your baby's likes and dislikes, she may become upset when you try to involve her in an activity that does not suit her mood at that particular moment.

● You may be trying to dress or bath her when she is hungry and crying for food. You might want to chat and play when she is overtired and just wants to sleep. This all takes time to learn, and in the meantime you need to judge your timing carefully.

● Consider her temperament, too. It will soon become clear whether she is easily startled by loud noises, sudden movements, bright lights or even too much cuddling, or whether she happily tolerates all of these things.

Emotional discomfort

All babies need the comfort and reassurance of being held close as often as possible in the early days. If you have ruled out all the potential physical causes of your baby's crying (see below, right), she probably needs soothing.

● **Insecurity** Your baby may settle quite happily in your arms or a sling, then be fretful when put down. This is a clear sign that she wants to be near you.

● **Boredom** As your baby gets older, from around five months,

she could be crying because she is bored and wants something – or someone – to amuse her. This could happen sooner if she's an active, wakeful baby (see pages 26–27).

● **Over-stimulation** Too much handling, noise, even play, can make your baby irritable and fretful.

● **Overtiredness** An overtired baby needs calm handling. To help relax her and soothe her so that she's able to go to sleep, try gentle rocking, singing, cuddling, stroking or sitting with her in a quiet, darkened room.

It's important to remember that:

● some babies prefer quiet, still times and very gentle handling, while others want more activity and may seem desperate to grow up

● some take heartily to feeding; others find it a struggle for a while

● some can be put down easily to settle after feeding; others will always complain and cry

● some babies may need to cry more to ensure that their higher demands for contact and care are met – a reminder that crying is also an attachment-promoting behaviour.

If your baby does seem to cry a lot, it is even more important to make the most of times when she is content to

CLOSE TO YOU
Your newborn baby loves the security of your arms, feeling the rhythm of your heartbeat and gazing into your smiling face.

Physical discomfort

There are many physical reasons why your baby could be crying.

● **Hunger** As soon as your baby feels hungry, she will cry to be fed. Before she starts to cry, look for early hunger signs, such as rooting, sucking and even opening and closing her hands over her chest.

● **Thirst** Newborn babies usually do not need extra fluids, other than their normal feeds. If your baby appears thirsty, try offering a little more.

● **A dirty or wet nappy** While needing a nappy change may not

observe, and interact with her (see pages 24–29). This will increase the bond between you, and give you good memories of the early days.

Your personality

If you are a naturally calm person, you may be better able to cope with crying than a more stressed parent would be. This is why individual parents' interpretations of crying vary – one may describe as excessive and unbearable crying that another finds challenging but possible to cope with.

All parents have been found to exaggerate the level of crying compared with that measured objectively by researchers on tape recordings. The reason for this is that a parent might say, "My baby has been crying for two hours", because for those two hours the baby has been awake, and fussing and crying intermittently. A recording may reveal only one hour of actual crying, but it feels like two hours of stress to parents who are combining the crying episodes as one long event.

Parents can also find different aspects of babycare more or less difficult. For example, one mother may enjoy relaxing when feeding her baby, while another feels it takes too long and is frustrated at being kept from jobs she thinks she should be doing around the house.

Your home life

Your personal circumstances will also have an impact on how easy it is for you to manage a crying baby. If you have the support of a partner, perhaps the experience of having had other children, or friends or family who can share the load with you, then you will probably manage more easily than a single or first-time mother with few friends or relatives living nearby.

If you are on your own, find out about mother-and-baby groups in your area – you will find the friendship and support you receive from meeting other mums an invaluable lifeline.

make every baby cry, leaving your baby in a wet or soiled nappy can aggravate her delicate skin.

● **Wind** Trapped wind can be uncomfortable. Keep her as upright as possible during a feed, and "wind" her by holding her against your shoulder and rubbing or patting her back.

● **Feeling too hot or too cold**
Young babies are not able to regulate their own temperature and need your help to make them feel comfortable. To check whether your baby is too hot (or too cold), feel her tummy not her hands or feet. Take off (or add) extra layers accordingly. Remove extra clothing from her when you come into a warm environment, even if she is asleep.

● **Needing a change of position**
Before she can shift her position by herself, your baby may cry for help if she is lying uncomfortably. Remember, however, that you must always lay her down to sleep on her back to avoid the risk of Sudden Infant Death Syndrome (SIDS).

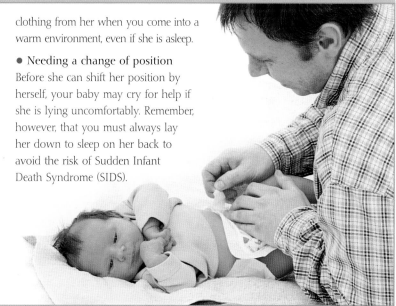

How can I comfort my newborn baby?

As you react to your baby's cry, your first thoughts are, "Why is she crying?" and, "How can I soothe her?" If there's no obvious physical cause for her crying (see page 14) , she'll need your help to calm down. Find out which comforting method works best for your baby and repeat it systematically. If one thing doesn't work, try several together – it's a question of trial and error.

Cuddles, contact and bonding

★ **Rocking in your arms** Research has shown that your heartbeat, rhythmical breathing pattern and regular movements help to establish a baby's own regular heart rate, respiratory and sleep patterns. You may find you instinctively sway your hips whenever you hold your baby close.

A DIFFERENT APPROACH
Don't worry if a tried-and-trusted method of soothing your baby seems not to work. It's worth persevering with other ways of comforting her until you find one that she can't resist.

TENDER LOVING CARE
Your warm embrace will usually prove to be irresistible to your newborn, helping her feel secure, loved and confident that you are there to meet her needs.

FEELING BETTER
As you rock her in your arms or hold her against your shoulder, watch for signs that her crying is subsiding and that she's ready to drop off to sleep.

★ **A sling** Carrying your baby in a sling can give comfort and closeness, as well as providing movement for her. It also leaves your hands free.

★ **Stroking** Gentle stroking of the forehead, or anywhere on your baby's body, may help her relax.

★ **Massage** This is the perfect way to soothe and bond with your baby (see pages 22–23). Soft stroking and massage is easy to do and both you and your baby will benefit from the intimacy.

Other ways to comfort

★ **Sounds and music** Anything from lullabies to pop songs can help. Also try recordings of womb sounds, or "white noise", the monotonous hum of the washing machine or vacuum cleaner.

★ **Going for a ride** You may rock your baby when she's in her pram or cradle and discover that she quietens because of the movement. Taking her out for a walk in her pram or pushchair, or a ride in the car, may also be effective for this reason. However, make sure that your baby doesn't come to rely on this as a way of getting to sleep – she needs to learn to do this by herself.

Feeding and crying

In the early weeks, it is normal for your baby to want to feed frequently – every two hours is not unusual. Small pre-term babies may need to feed even more often than this to catch up with their growing. Often they are awake more at night and want to sleep all day.

There are several reasons why your newborn needs frequent feeds.

● Breast milk is perfect food for your newborn, but it is low in fat and protein, so she digests it quickly and easily and is soon hungry again.

● Your newborn has a tiny stomach, so "little and often" is best for her.

● It takes time for both you and your baby to learn how to breastfeed efficiently.

● Remember also that breastfeeding works on a "supply-and-demand" basis, so that as your baby sucks, your breasts are stimulated into

"We both get so much out of breastfeeding. It helps me relax, and I know I'm giving him the best possible start."

MELISSA is mum to 12-week-old Daniel

making more milk for the next feed. To keep up with demand, ensure that you eat a nutritious diet, and drink plenty of fluids. This is especially important when you feel you need to increase your milk supply.

● Trying to feed your newborn baby by the clock will inevitably lead to a lot more crying as it takes several weeks for her feeding to settle into a routine.

Sleeping and crying

In the beginning, your baby doesn't really know the difference between night and day, and it is better to accept your baby's rhythms and routines for now. Trying to fit your baby into an imaginary schedule at this stage will lead to more crying.

Helping your baby

After the first few months, however, it is worth thinking about sleep routines, and you can begin to set up bedtime rituals, such as a bath, a cuddle and a story, in the evening. These are signals that even tiny babies start to recognize.

Even for daytime naps, by about four months it is worth putting your baby down at set times, and in a recognizable way if you can, preferably in the cot in her bedroom.

Sleep facts

It is important to remember that:

● a baby's internal body clock is not fully developed until at least six weeks

● babies' sleep patterns are quite different from those of adults. They spend much longer in light, active REM (rapid-eye-movement) sleep when they are more likely to wake – 50 per cent of the time compared with 25 per cent in adults

● premature babies spend even more time in light sleep

● it is not until six months or more that a baby's brain regulates sleep in a similar way to adults.

The benefits of swaddling

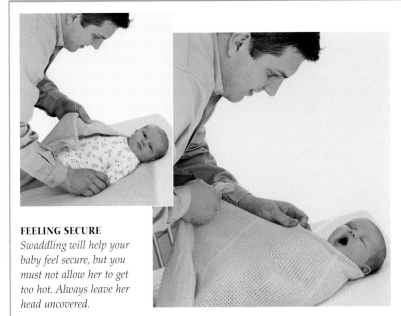

FEELING SECURE
Swaddling will help your baby feel secure, but you must not allow her to get too hot. Always leave her head uncovered.

Wrapping your newborn quite firmly, "papoose style", in a light blanket or sheet could help to calm her, especially if she's sensitive and easily startled. Many babies are upset by the jerking movements of their limbs, and swaddling prevents this happening.

Fold the blanket or sheet and lay your baby on top of it. Her neck should be level with the fold. Bring one side of the blanket over her body and tuck it firmly under her. Then do the same with the other side. Tuck the end of the blanket under her feet and legs. You may wrap her arms, or leave them free so that she can get them to her mouth to soothe herself.

Checklist

When it feels as though your young baby's crying is getting on top of you, take a break (see pages 36–41). The following facts may help you to put things into perspective.

- It is not possible to spoil a baby by going to her when she cries.

- Your newborn is never just "exercising her lungs".

- Her crying is a reflex to express needs or to get help when she can't cope alone with the overwhelming changes in her world.

- Your newborn never cries to manipulate you. She is using the only language she has at the beginning to ensure that her needs are met.

Meeting her needs – fast!

There is a great deal of evidence that the more quickly you can meet your baby's cries in the early days, by going immediately to respond to her, you will be helping to build a feeling of greater security and confidence. As a result, your baby is less likely to cry excessively later on. There is also a developmental reason for not leaving your newborn to cry for too long.

Being loving and responsive in the early days can actually help your baby's brain develop, and lead to better language development. Having said that, many babies fuss or cry for a short time when first put down, so you may need to leave her for a few minutes to settle – but never more than five minutes for a new baby.

Take a realistic view

It helps if you can have a realistic view of what having a baby is really like. This can be difficult when we see everywhere images of perfectly contented, smiling babies, being cared for by parents who appear to be totally relaxed and confident in their role. Some parents may have had no chance to learn that the reality may sometimes be like that, but there will also be many challenges to face.

The attitude of others may not help the assumption that a "good"

baby doesn't cry, and a "good" parent can always solve crying. Neither of these things is true.

If you are becoming very upset by your new baby's crying, someone less emotionally involved, such as your partner, may be able to soothe her more easily. This is not a reflection on you – your baby's behaviour is not related to you being a bad mother, nor is it because she doesn't like you. She can react to your tension, so you must share the care and find ways to relax (see page 41).

Involving dads

Research shows lots of benefits when dads are fully involved with the day-to-day care of their babies. Their emotional support in the early days is vital, and will make a big difference to you, especially while you are getting breastfeeding established successfully.

Your partner can also play a key role in the early emotional development of your baby. He will create loving bonds by carrying out all the same physical and emotional care that you do.

It's also important that you involve your partner right from the beginning. Not only will his help give you a break, it also prevents him feeling that he's missing out on caring for your baby or that you are so involved with her, you no longer have any time left over for him.

Even if you are breastfeeding your baby, there are many other ways your partner can get involved. He can still cuddle, "wind", bath, change nappies and comfort her when she's crying. He can carry her in a sling, and take her out for a walk in the pram or pushchair. Dads are just as

capable of doing all the practical babycare activities as you are, and can be an equally hands-on parent. The more opportunities they have to hold and cuddle their babies, the more confident and relaxed they become, and the closer their bond. Everyone gains from it.

SOFT AND GENTLE
Your newborn is likely to be soothed by the soft feel of a fleece against her delicate skin. But be careful not to let her sleep on a fleece because of the risk of suffocation.

Self-comforting

Sucking is the most obvious source of comfort for all crying babies. Your newborn can suck the breast, bottle or a dummy, or you can help her to try to find her own fist or your clean fingers. Although it is well known that babies suck their thumbs in the womb, it will be two or three months before they really learn to suck their thumbs effectively.

Can massage help ease my baby's crying?

Baby massage can be relaxing and beneficial for both babies and parents. Through eye contact and touch, it promotes bonding and boosts your baby's confidence and wellbeing. There is even evidence that it can reduce crying levels and relieve "colic", encourage better sleep patterns and possibly help boost your baby's immune system. Massage is generally recommended for healthy full-term babies. It is also better not to massage your baby if she seems ill or has had a recent immunization. Baby massage classes are an ideal way to learn the techniques – and to make new friends. Your health visitor should have information.

Massaging tips

★ You can massage your baby when she's undressed or through her clothes.
★ Make sure that the room is warm.
★ Your hands should be clean and warm. You may like to use baby oil (avoid aromatherapy and nut-based oils).
★ Pay attention to your baby's cues that she is enjoying the massage. Some babies find it stimulating; others like only one part of their body massaged.
★ Massage is best in between feeds, not just after or just before one.

HER HEAD AND SHOULDERS
Using the tips of your fingers or thumb, gently stroke your baby's forehead out to her temple, then her neck to her shoulders. If she's alert, keep eye contact, talk softly and smile at her.

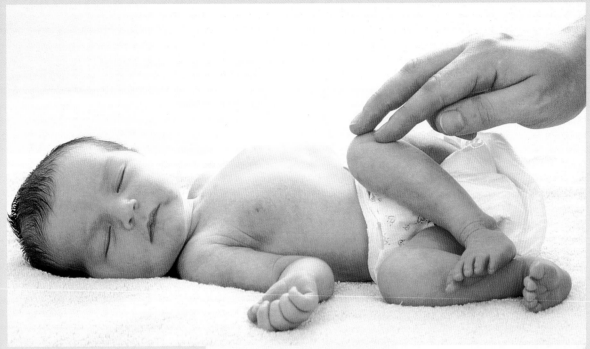

HER LEGS

Making small circular strokes with your fingertips, or gently squeezing with your hand, massage down from her thighs to her knees, and then down her shins to her ankles. You could work one leg at a time or both simultaneously.

HER HANDS AND ARMS

From her shoulders, continue your strokes down along her arm to her hand. Again, you could work on one limb at a time or both together. Next, try some very gentle circular strokes on her tummy, using one hand.

HER FEET

Working down her legs, massage her ankles, her feet and finally each of her toes. You could finish by gently cycling her legs.

*" Ralph has always been very alert. He's still so young and yet he seems **interested** in everything that's going on **around him**. It's as though he doesn't want to miss a thing. "*

PETER is dad to eight-week-old Ralph

3

Getting to know your baby

Comforting your baby is not just about finding ways to quieten him once he's started crying. Often, you may be able to step in and pre-empt his crying simply by learning to recognize potential triggers, spotting and responding to cues that he is about to change "state", and being sensitive to his moods and individual nature.

It was once thought that babies didn't really know what was going on around them. We now understand that this is far from true, and that babies arrive with amazing talents.

Six states

To begin with, you may think that your baby has only a few recognizable ways of behaving. You would certainly count crying and sleeping among them, but researchers have studied babies closely to identify six distinct "states", even in the newborn. These states depend on how wakeful the baby is, and are:

- quiet sleep
- active sleep
- drowsiness
- quiet alert
- active alert
- crying.

It sometimes seems impossible to believe, but new babies do spend most time in the sleep state – the average is 16 hours in 24 hours. This alternates between quiet, peaceful sleep and light, active (REM or rapid-eye-movement) sleep – about half of the time in each.

In contrast, the average time spent crying daily is only about two hours, and even excessive crying

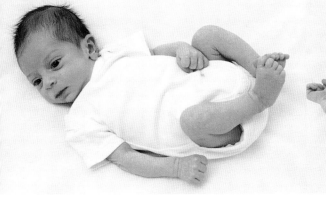

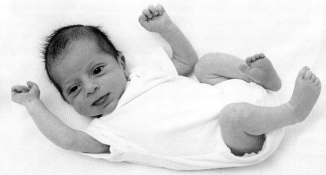

QUIET ALERT
The quiet alert state is probably the best time to get to know your baby. He will be content and relaxed, perhaps because he is fresh from a sleep, and ready to interact with you.

ACTIVE ALERT
This is an early warning sign that your baby is about to want something, perhaps a feed or some attention from you. Help him by noticing this change in him, and quickly meet his needs.

Comforting to suit your baby's temperament

To comfort an easily over-stimulated baby:

• create a calm environment for him and keep lights dim

• keep play sessions brief, and watch for cues that he's had enough – he may turn his head away or squeeze his eyes shut

• encourage sucking – a fist, thumb or a dummy should help

• try lying down in a darkened room with your baby on your chest

• avoid handling by many different people

• ensure, as much as possible, that his naps are at home and in his Moses basket, cradle or cot.

To comfort a sensitive baby:

• do all you can to cut down triggers, such as sudden cold or loud noises

• watch for cues that he's about to cry (becoming tense or jerking his body)

• speak in a soothing voice, telling him you understand his distress

• take things slowly and at your baby's pace – for example, never rush feeding

• use soft cotton clothes and covers for his sensitive skin

• if bathing or undressing him adds to his distress, keep it to a minimum

• use distraction from frustrations as your baby grows (see pages 50–51).

To comfort an active baby:

• put him in a baby chair, so that he can see more from his propped-up position. Swings and bouncers are also useful

• keep chatting to him while you are working around the house

• move him to different rooms and views to provide variety

• provide lots of stimulating things to look at, such as mobiles

• plenty of songs and games work well

• make regular changes of playthings, so that he doesn't become bored

• set up his toys in different areas of the house so you can keep him interested.

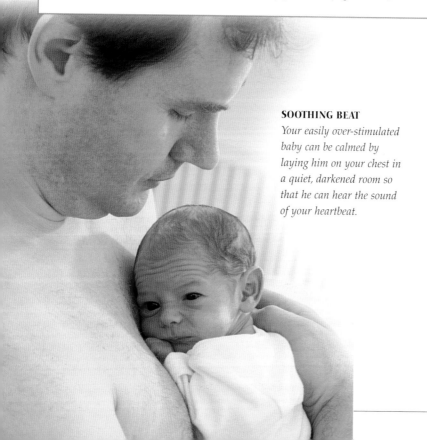

SOOTHING BEAT
Your easily over-stimulated baby can be calmed by laying him on your chest in a quiet, darkened room so that he can hear the sound of your heartbeat.

may only be about three or four hours. So, looking on the bright side, your baby will be crying a lot less than sleeping!

The quiet alert state is probably the most interesting state for parents. To begin with, new babies spend only about 2½ hours in 24 in this state, but this is the time to communicate and "play" with your baby, cooing, gazing or smiling at him.

The active alert state is when your baby wants to eat, or may be "fussy" and wanting your attention, while drowsiness is best described as the intermediate state, when your baby is either falling asleep or just waking up.

Different temperaments

All babies show these behaviours, but the way in which they move from one state to the other differs greatly. Some can be brought very easily to the quiet alert state, while for others this is a lot harder. Researchers have studied different types of temperament, and while your baby may not fit neatly into one category or another, it can be reassuring to know why your baby behaves the way he does, and may help you to prevent or soothe his crying.

● **An easily over-stimulated baby** may cry without an obvious explanation, just because sights or sounds that have been fascinating to him for a while suddenly become too much.

● **A sensitive baby** may cry when undressed or bathed, and will probably howl at procedures such as being examined by a doctor. As all babies get older, they cry from frustration at not being able to do things, but the sensitive baby is easily frustrated and so cries all the more.

● **An active baby** needs to have plenty of attention. He may be awake a lot during the day and appear to take great interest in his surroundings, virtually from birth.

LOOK AND LEARN
A fun mobile over your active baby's cot will entertain him, and help keep crying at bay. For safety, take down the mobile before he's able to sit up.

Spotting pre-crying signals

Once you understand about each one of your baby's states, his temperament and how that affects the way in which he's able to make the transition from one state to another, you can often begin to anticipate early warning signs, such as turning away or closing his eyes, to demonstrate that he is about to become over-loaded or over-stimulated. Other signals to look out for include:

● rubbing his eyes
● making sucking noises
● starting to "root" around.

   Being able to spot these cues from your baby can enable you to pre-empt his crying. You could also think about changing situations that always seem to lead to crying. If, for example, you notice that your baby cries a lot after being cuddled by visitors, keep this to a minimum or take him to a quieter room.

Also, through watching your baby carefully, you will probably see how he uses self-soothing techniques to move himself to a more comfortable relaxed state. As well as sucking (see page 21), he may also:

• put a hand to his mouth
• begin to stare at something
• change position – turning his body or head from one side to the other.

Some babies use all of these skills easily. Others find the effort overwhelming and need more help from their parents.

Reassuring advice

In the 1970s, American paediatrician T. Berry Brazelton worked out a method of assessing newborn behaviour, which may be used by healthcare professionals to determine how soon babies will cry in response to various triggers, such as noise or light, and then how easy or difficult they are to console.

All the guilt we sometimes feel as parents – that it is somehow our fault that our baby cries, that we are not giving the right kind of care – seems less when we realize that our baby may just be reacting to the

Consoling your crying baby

T. Berry Brazelton devised the following sequence to console a crying baby. The time it takes varies from one baby to another, and it probably won't work if your baby is already crying hard or very hungry.

You may do all of these things in an effort to console your baby already, but most likely you use them in a more random way. It is certainly worth trying them in a calm, structured sequence.

1 Bring your face close to your baby so she can see you.

2 Maintaining eye contact with your baby, speak quietly and calmly to her. It is not really important what you say to her, but do remember to use her name regularly.

3 Place a hand firmly on her tummy, keeping up the eye contact and still using a soft voice.

4 Hold your baby's arms very gently to her side, so that she can't wave them around.

5 Pick up your baby and cuddle her.

6 Hold your baby up against your shoulder, so that she can look around from there.

7 Help your baby to suck her own fist or thumb or your clean fingers, or give her a dummy.

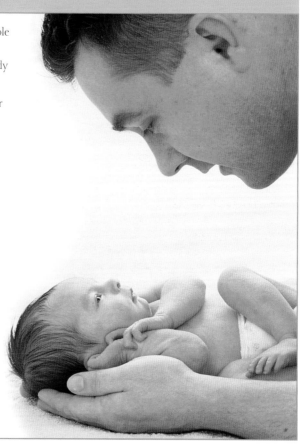

Using a dummy

Only you can weigh up the pros and cons of using dummies. As long as they are kept clean, and regularly checked for safety, it is an individual choice for you and your baby. The ideal may be to use one only in the early months, taking it away before your baby comes to depend on it.

In the early months, dummies must be sterilized. But once your baby starts moving around and putting all sorts of other things in his mouth, sterilizing is pointless.

Never dip your baby's dummies in anything sweet as this can damage his emerging teeth.

If your baby is still using a dummy at six months, you could provide a security object, such as a blanket or soft toy, then gradually limit dummy use between nine and 12 months.

The pros
- A dummy can be an effective way of soothing your baby and can help him settle back to sleep at night.
- It's easier to wean your baby off a dummy than a thumb – thumbs are always within easy reach.

The cons
- Dummies are easy to lose and this can cause a lot of distress – especially at night, when your baby will cry for you to help find it for him.
- It may be hard to wean your child off it, even for years afterwards.
- As your baby gets older, using a dummy can cut down the opportunities to make babbling pre-vocal sounds and slow down speech development.

Questions & Answers

I have noticed that my nine-month-old daughter likes to settle down with the corner of a blanket in her hand. Should I encourage this?
In the early days, you were your baby's favourite "comforter". But from around eight months, many babies become very attached to so-called "transitional" comfort objects. This could be a dummy, but often it is a soft toy or bits of cloth or a blanket, all of which are soft to the touch and smell familiar, and are therefore comforting to your baby. This is perfectly normal and should be encouraged, because it will help her to settle herself to sleep, and comfort her if she's feeling upset or insecure.

noise from the radio or light from the window in his eyes. It can help simply to understand how babies can use their behaviour to deal with their environment, by crying, calming down, waking up or sleeping, interacting with caregivers or "tuning out" things they don't like.

But ideally, of course, the purpose of the assessment is to demonstrate to parents just how unique their baby is, how amazingly capable all newborns are, and to promote their relationship with one another in a positive way.

" Chloe has worked out quite well now how to suck her thumb, and she does this to comfort herself when she's tired, and often when she's just taking a look around at what's going on. "

MAE is mum to five-month-old Chloe

" Monty had bouts of **inconsolable** crying until he was 14 weeks old. He'd throw himself back and scream. My husband and I are quite laid-back, but even so, it was hard at times. He's **happy now.** "

SOPHIE is mum to seven-month-old Monty

4

Unexplained and inconsolable crying

Many parents and health professionals describe excessive crying as "colic". Recent findings, based on research evidence, indicate that there is no physiological cause for colic. So, rather than look for causes and cures, think of it as an extreme form of normal crying that will end of its own accord by the third or fourth month, and concentrate on ways of comforting your baby.

So, what is "colic"?

"Colic" is a distressing pattern of crying that is at the end of the spectrum of normal crying, and is something babies "do", rather than something they "have". Colic is not an "illness" in itself, and in the vast majority of cases there is no underlying medical cause.

Having said that, it is important that you consult your doctor if you are at all worried about your baby, so that he can rule out any health problems and reassure you that your baby is well. Illness or pain, including colds, ear infections or urinary infections, can all cause colic-like crying, so it is always a good idea to rule them out (see pages 58–61).

Researchers defined colic in 1954 as: "Paroxysms of irritability, fussing or crying, lasting for a total of more than three hours a day, and occurring on more than three days in any week in a young infant less than three months of age." This is sometimes called the "Rule of three".

According to this definition, probably only about 10 per cent of babies up to three months are colicky, although estimates as high as 85 per cent have been inaccurately quoted.

A crying puzzle

Unexplained, and often inconsolable, crying is unusual in that it does not fit well with the idea that babies cry in order to have a need met. You may try everything, and yet your baby still cries.

In fact, it has been shown that, despite crying excessively, babies

Checklist

"Colic" crying has some distinctive characteristics.

- It usually starts when your baby's around two to three weeks old.

- It is worse at certain times, often late afternoon or early evening.

- It seems to start for no reason and goes on for long periods, during which it can be difficult to console your baby.

- The crying sometimes seems worse after feeding.

- Your baby often pulls up her legs, arches her back, or goes red in the face when crying.

- It subsides at three to four months.

Questions & Answers

Is "colic" the same thing as excessive crying?

Excessive crying may not fit the patterns and definitions of colic. It can last longer than three months, and may not follow the evening peak pattern. It happens at different times of day, or occasionally lasts for what seems like all day – or all night. Help your baby by starting to establish a sleep/wake routine, so that his world is structured and predictable and to avoid overtiredness. Give him sensitive care according to his temperament, and try to intercept before crying starts.

do not have body changes that might be expected. Their heart rates and cortisol levels – a chemical in the blood that is an indicator of stress – may remain within the normal range, even when crying their hardest!

This type of crying could even be considered to be a lot like sleep difficulties, in that it is a problem, *but not for your baby.* It is the effect these behaviours have on you,

COMFORTING HOLD
A baby with colic may be soothed by being held in a position that allows gentle pressure on her abdomen.

her parents, that is the real issue.

Hold onto the fact that this phase will pass soon, usually around three to four months, and will have no lasting effects on your baby. A colicky baby will not become a more difficult toddler or child.

Medical concerns

In the past, it has been suggested that colic could be the result of a problem with a baby's immature

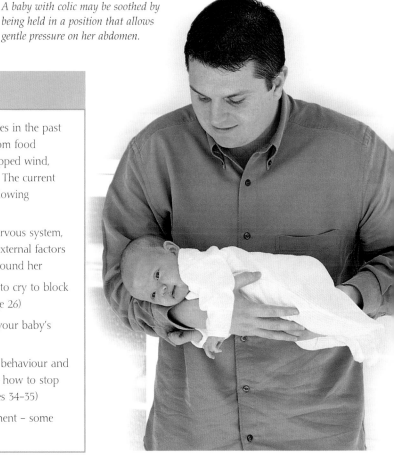

What are the causes?

There have been many unproven theories in the past over what may be the cause of colic, from food intolerances and parental tension, to trapped wind, and evening hunger in breastfed babies. The current thinking about colic crying gives the following possible explanations:

● your baby may have an immature nervous system, especially if she seems very reactive to external factors – lights, sounds or activities going on around her

● she may be a sensitive baby, needing to cry to block out other distressing sensations (see page 26)

● crying at the end of the day may be your baby's way of releasing tension

● she is having difficulty regulating her behaviour and once she starts crying she doesn't know how to stop – she needs your help to settle (see pages 34–35)

● it's all down to your baby's temperament – some babies simply cry more than others.

"Amir has just turned three months old and his colic is completely gone. He is much more cheerful, and easier to settle. We can relax in the evenings now!"

SUNITA is mum to three-month-old Amir

Expert tips

Try the following when you are coping with a colicky baby.

• Take it in turns with your partner to care for your baby and get as much help and support as possible from friends and relatives to give yourself a break.

• Try to identify a pattern to the crying, by keeping a diary (see page 60). It can help you feel more in control and is useful for health professionals, too.

• Talk to other parents who have been through the same experience or call a helpline, such as Cry-sis (see page 62).

• Keep reminding yourself that colic lasts for a relatively short period. It is not worth getting too upset or worn out trying to find "cures".

• Focus on every positive moment with your baby. Keep a diary of these, too, so you can see that there are good times as well as bad.

central nervous or gastrointestinal system. Feeding difficulties, or perhaps a dietary intolerance of some kind, often to cows' milk protein, have also been put forward as possible causes.

Recent research has concluded, however, that it would be in only a small minority, possibly about 10 per cent of cases, that digestive problems could cause this extreme form of crying. Yet, parents are often told, as the first response, to change their method of feeding.

However, colic occurs more or less equally in bottle-fed and breastfed babies, so realistically, any change would have an effect on only a small number of colicky babies. The concern is that mothers of perfectly healthy babies may decide to give up breastfeeding earlier than they had intended, make frequent, unnecessary changes in the milk formula they are using, or be tempted to introduce solid foods too soon.

Waiting it out

If your baby is healthy and has been found to be developing well at all the regular health checks, it would be realistic to accept that even the *best* improvement that it is possible to obtain in most cases of colic may not be remarkable. All your efforts to soothe your baby may modify the crying only slightly, although even a few minutes' respite is often better than nothing.

Hang on to the fact that *all* crying goes down after three or four months. Even though babies who are excessive criers may cry more than other babies until at least five months, they will be crying much less than before.

How can I comfort my baby with colic?

Even though you try your best to keep a positive attitude throughout your baby's extreme crying bouts and fervently hold on to the fact that it will end in a few weeks, you probably feel happier trying something – anything! – to comfort your baby, if only for a short while.

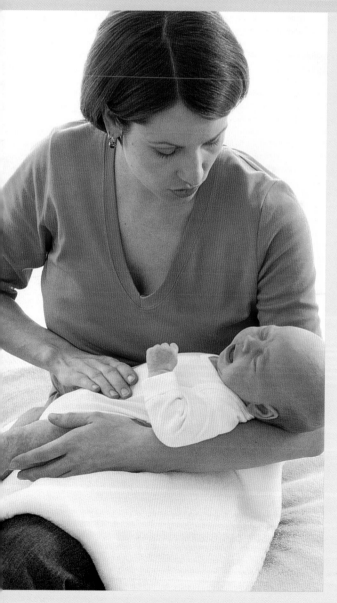

Physical contact

Remember, babies who have more physical contact may cry less. The benefits of cuddles and stroking have a well-proven physiological basis, and even when your baby's crying is not soothed, you may be boosting her immune system and growth hormones. Physical contact is always worthwhile.

It's also worth trying all the usual comfort tips for crying, such as sucking, rocking, playing music or singing, and massage (see pages 16-17). They may help for a while – but don't be surprised if, after a brief lull, your baby starts crying again. Find the three to five most successful strategies and rotate them through in the same order.

Soothing techniques

Other comforting tips to consider trying include:
★ doing a "colic dance", in which you rock your baby up and down while swaying your hips from side to side

GENTLE PRESSURE ON HER TUMMY
Holding your baby in the crook of your arm, place your hand on your baby's tummy and rub it gently. At the same time, maintain eye contact and talk to her softly, using her name regularly.

★ applying gentle pressure to your baby's tummy, such as in the Brazelton technique (see page 28)

★ holding your baby in positions that allow pressure on her abdomen, for example over your knees, across the crook of your arm or upright against your shoulder

★ applying warmth to your baby's tummy, such as the gentle heat from a covered hot-water bottle filled with warm – not hot – water held against her through her clothes

★ giving her a bath – but do be sensitive to your baby's temperament. Some colicky babies find a bath soothing, while others are more agitated by it

★ winding your baby – try keeping her as upright as possible during feeds, or break off from a feed, hold her against your shoulder and gently rub her back to help her to bring the wind up

★ using homeopathic remedies, such as colocynthis, or herbal drinks, such as fennel or chamomile. *Always* consult a qualified practitioner who specializes in treating babies and children before giving any complementary remedies

★ trying cranial osteopathy (see page 61), which may help if your baby has misaligned skull bones following birth. Again, always use a qualified practitioner (see page 62).

FACE DOWN
Holding your baby in the crook of your arm allows you to apply gentle pressure to her tummy, while swaying her from side to side. She'll feel secure as her body is supported along the length of your arm, and the movement may also distract and soothe her.

PAT HER BACK
When you feel confident with this position, and have a secure hold on the thigh of her leg furthest from your body, use your free hand to pat gently or rub her back using circular movements.

"Edward's crying has affected **the whole family**. When Henry and Robyn are trying to do their homework, I reassure them that **this stage will soon pass**, and take Edward upstairs to soothe him."

MAGGIE is grandmother to three-month-old Edward, Robyn, 14, and Henry, 11

Crying and its impact on family life

Family lives are often complex. As a first-time parent, you can concentrate solely on learning about and caring for your baby. Later, as your family grows, you may find yourself with a baby, a demanding toddler and a child just starting school. You now have a diverse set of relationships to manage, as well as your baby's crying.

A baby in the family

Real family life is very different from the glossy version that we see on television or read about in magazines. If you have a crying baby and older children with equally important needs to be met, you may have to explore a range of solutions in order to keep going some of the essential activities of your normal family routine.

You need to discover what works best for your whole family, and this will vary with how many children you have, their ages and temperaments, as well as all your other circumstances.

It is important for all of you to hang on to the fact that these changes in family dynamics are to be expected for a while, and that things will soon return to normal.

Your older children

A baby who cries excessively or inconsolably is bound to affect every member of the family in some way. When a baby arrives, it's a time of very mixed emotions. Younger children may themselves associate crying with occasions when they have been unhappy or have hurt themselves, and can be quite upset by the idea that their baby may be feeling sad.

Older children may not relate to the crying in quite the same way, but may find that it interferes with their routines and feel that they are missing out on a good deal of their parents' attention.

Checklist

Help your other children by:

- encouraging them to talk about their feelings

- sympathizing with them about how distracting the crying can be, reassuring them that this period will not last very long, and that soon you will have more time for them again

- thinking of ways to give them undivided attention. Perhaps your partner could play with your toddler more, or you could settle down to read to her while you feed the baby

- involving your children as much as possible in helping to amuse or calm the baby. Turn it into a family project!

- taking up all offers of help. Going to the cinema with a grandparent or a sleepover with a friend will be a welcome treat for older children.

" My older children have been so helpful, which is good because I find the more time I can spend comforting Orin, the more relaxed we all are."

FRAN is mum to two-week-old Orin

All siblings may be annoyed or even angry at the many challenges a new baby brings. But then they are also likely to feel guilty about or be unable to understand these negative thoughts.

Be positive

You will inevitably have some guilty moments over how your older children's lives have changed with the arrival of a new baby, and feel yourself pulled in all directions. But

don't allow guilt to take away the time your baby needs from you to feel secure. The more you are able to respond to your baby, allowing him to claim your attention so that you learn how to soothe him, the less he will cry in a few months and the happier everyone in the family will be.

Getting help

Never be afraid to ask for help, and take up all offers from your partner, grandparents, other family members or friends.

- Talk to other parents – they have all been there! Find out if there are any postnatal groups you can join in your area.

- Talk to your healthcare professional for general advice and support – particularly if you feel you're beginning to find it hard to cope (see page 60).

- Look on the internet for parent support groups, or see *Useful Contacts* on page 62.

Always remember that your baby's crying is not your fault, and it is not a reflection on your abilities as a parent either.

Be confident

Try to feel confident enough to ignore unhelpful advice about how other people manage crying, when the tone and implication are that you are getting it wrong.

You're tired, and probably stressed, and thoughtless remarks won't help matters. Some grandparents, for example, who naturally have high expectations of their new grandchild, may be disappointed if he regularly cries when handed to them, and so feel they can offer advice on ways of raising babies that have gone out of fashion – "In my day, we wouldn't have put up with all this crying – you're spoiling him." With the best intentions, they may genuinely think that you are doing something wrong, and this can cause conflict.

If you feel up to it, tactfully explain that you believe individual babies need different types of care and that you are doing the best you can for your baby.

The best type of help you need at the moment is from someone who can provide practical support, giving

Expert tips

- Be as honest as you can about how the baby's crying is making everybody feel. It can be hard to express negative thoughts, because the social pressures are so great to pretend that everything is perfect when a new baby arrives. But it can really help everybody to feel relieved that these thoughts and feelings are normal and will pass.

- Consider separate beds or bedrooms for a while so that you and your partner each have the much-needed chance to catch up on sleep and rest. Take turns spending nights with the baby – obviously you won't have this option if you are breastfeeding, unless you express some milk, but even a few hours' unbroken sleep can be restful.

- Talk things through with your family, and draw up lists of what absolutely needs to be done, and who can do what. Older children may surprise you with their sensible suggestions and offers of help.

- Ask older children to help you keep a diary of your baby's crying (see page 60) – they will feel important to be given the task, and you may all be amazed to find that the crying lasts for less time than you thought.

- Keep your sense of humour – just pulling a funny face and saying to your toddler, "Oh no, here we go again!" when the baby starts to cry may lighten everybody's mood.

Questions & Answers

How can I keep my toddler and six-year-old busy when the baby is crying?
The following ideas may help.

- Play a favourite video or music tape.

- Ask them to draw you a picture – even if it's of the baby crying!

- Provide a toy phone and ask your toddler to phone Daddy or Granny to tell them about the baby's crying.

- Give your older child some colourful catalogues and ask her to tear out any toys she would like next birthday or Christmas.

- Enlist their help, rocking a cradle, pushing a pram to the park.

- Arrange visits for them to friends.

you a break by taking the baby for a while, or emotional support as a non-judgemental listening ear.

Your relationship

With so many demands on your time, it is inevitable that you and your partner put your relationship low on your list of priorities. But it's important that your baby's crying does not start to affect your relationship.

Even five minutes a day, catching up over a cup of coffee will make a difference to how you both feel and

your ability to cope. A night out, leaving trusted friends or relatives to look after your children, will help even more.

Take a break

When you've tried everything, and the crying still won't end, you need a break. Put your baby safely in his Moses basket or cot and leave him for a few moments to have some time to yourself. Make a cup of tea, lie down quietly and do some deep breathing. Don't go back to your baby until you feel calm again.

HELPING HANDS
Whether you have twins or just one to care for, the help of your partner, or a grandparent, will give you a well-earned rest.

What about me?

The urgent nature of a baby's cries guarantees that everything else takes second place – especially your own needs. However, you must be uncompromising about the importance of looking after yourself if you are doing most of the caring for a crying baby. Without some nurturing and breaks, it is hard to keep going. Also, if you are relaxed and happy, the crying will never seem as bad. So by meeting your own needs, you'll be helping your baby, too.

Stress-busting tips

★ Eat a healthy balanced diet, especially if you are breastfeeding. Fruit, cheese, carrot sticks or raisins can all easily be eaten as snacks.

★ Find any way possible to get enough sleep. Use times when your baby is asleep to take a nap yourself, or at least rest with your feet up and a good book or magazine to read.

★ Keep household chores to the bare minimum. Prioritize jobs that really have to be done, such as washing the baby's clothes, and leave those that can wait. If possible, get some help around the house.

★ Go for a brisk walk with your baby. The fresh air and change of scenery will do both of you good.

★ Leave your partner or a relative in charge and go out with some friends – even an hour or two's break will give you a boost.

★ Take some exercise. Look for a gym or fitness club that has a crèche, or join a postnatal exercise class that you can do with your baby. It's a good opportunity to make friends, too.

★ Learn some relaxation techniques, such as slow,

TIME OUT
Use the precious hours when your baby is asleep to take time out for yourself. Catch up on your sleep, lose yourself in a good book, listen to some soothing music or relax in the bath.

deep breathing, meditation, yoga or self-massage.

★ Find some "treats" for yourself every day – someone bringing a drink while you are feeding the baby, a leisurely soak in the bath or the chance to go for a swim while someone else cares for the baby – whatever works best for you.

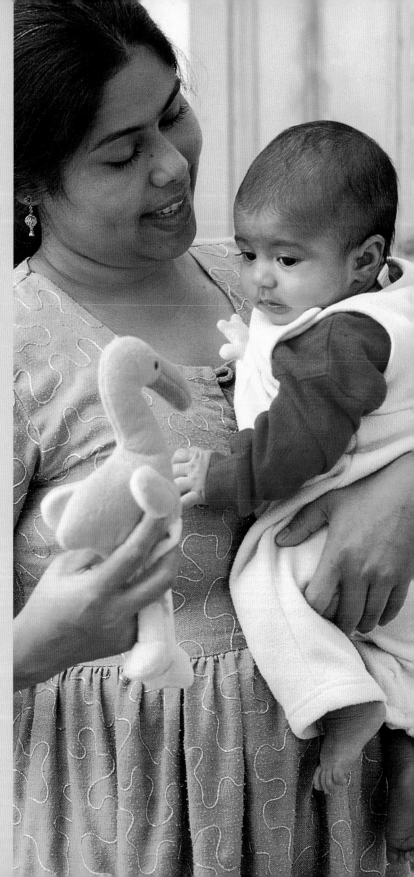

" Natasha doesn't like being left alone – that always makes her cry. I **comfort her** by picking her up and rubbing her back, and saying, **'It's okay,'** then I find something to amuse her. "

JENNIFER is mum to four-month-old Natasha

6

Crying in older babies

From around three months of age, your baby will begin to cry less. Even those babies who have cried excessively, and may continue to cry more for a little longer, will soon start to show signs of settling down. You're more confident because you are more in tune with your baby, and have many effective ways of soothing her.

A turning point

Many babies do just grow out of crying excessively, often by approximately three to four months. This is partly related to your baby's development – she's now becoming more sociable and is able to do more, such as grasp a toy or roll over.

It is also because your older baby is more adept at finding ways of soothing herself, such as being able to find her own thumb to suck or becoming attached to a "transitional" comfort object (see page 29).

It is true that few babies, who did not seem to cry excessively in the early days, begin to cry more around five to six months. This may be caused by teething or distress at the introduction of solid foods. It is also a possibility that they need to cry more to ensure more interaction with their parents, who may have been providing them

with less attention because they had seemed so much more settled! Either way, you have learned so much over the last few months about handling your baby, finding out her likes and dislikes, that you now deal easily with her needs. You have a better understanding of the different patterns of her crying. You will probably have many effective ways of comforting her.

More good news!

By the time your baby is three months, family life is settling into a more comfortable routine. You know how you can keep her happy a lot more of the time, and it's rewarding when she takes an interest in toys, or watches you contentedly from a sitting position while you carry out jobs around the house. This in turn means that there is a much wider range of activities you can try to calm her when she does cry.

Checklist

All babies cry less from three months. This is partly developmental, but also it is because:

- she's taking an interest in the world around her, so there's more to see and do
- she's more active and is busy developing her motor skills
- she's more sociable and is better able to interact with you and other caregivers
- you know your baby well by now and can recognize her crying triggers
- you have more effective ways of soothing her crying.

Why older babies cry

Hunger, over-stimulation and overtiredness are still likely causes for your older baby's crying. You will probably be familiar with the signs to look out for now and be ready to comfort her.

However, there are now a number of new reasons why your older baby cries.

● Crying for attention

Older babies can cry intentionally, because they want you to come to them, and then act pleased to see you. It is wrong to think of this as "naughty" or your baby manipulating you. She still uses crying as a means of communicating her needs and emotions. Also, there is no one in the world as important to your baby as you. She wants to spend time with you, and demonstrates this by squealing with delight whenever you come to her. This is part of the magic of parenting.

● Starting solid foods

You may notice more crying at mealtimes when your baby is trying her first solids from around six months. This could be because your baby simply dislikes the new feeding experience, or the taste of the food. She may reject a cup or spoon, or object to having to wait for her milk after her meal.

● Boredom

The chances of your baby feeling bored can increase as she grows older and spends less time sleeping during the day, so that bouncers, toys, mobiles and your company all become increasingly important to keep her occupied for parts of the day.

● Anxiety and fright

Your older baby may start to worry about things that never bothered her before. Typically, it may be the sound of the vacuum cleaner, or the sight of an animal, or having her hair washed that starts the crying.

Even if these fears seem trivial to you, you must not let her know that.

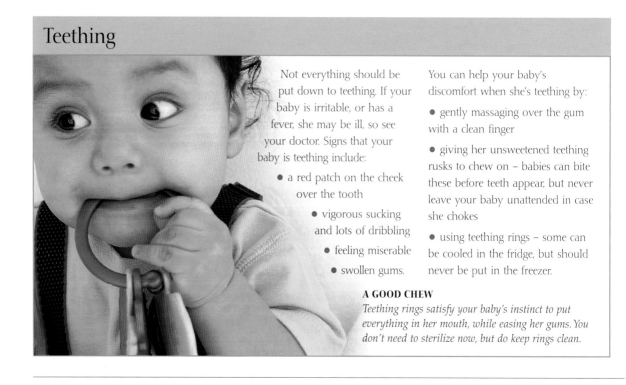

Teething

Not everything should be put down to teething. If your baby is irritable, or has a fever, she may be ill, so see your doctor. Signs that your baby is teething include:

● a red patch on the cheek over the tooth

● vigorous sucking and lots of dribbling

● feeling miserable

● swollen gums.

You can help your baby's discomfort when she's teething by:

● gently massaging over the gum with a clean finger

● giving her unsweetened teething rusks to chew on – babies can bite these before teeth appear, but never leave your baby unattended in case she chokes

● using teething rings – some can be cooled in the fridge, but should never be put in the freezer.

A GOOD CHEW
Teething rings satisfy your baby's instinct to put everything in her mouth, while easing her gums. You don't need to sterilize now, but do keep rings clean.

Separation anxiety

Having spent all the early months of her life becoming attached to you, it is very common for your baby not to want to let you out of her sight from about seven to eight months. Often this new behaviour coincides with the time when you need to introduce childcare for the first time, perhaps because you are returning to work.

Some babies will be more "clingy" than others, considering everyone other than Mummy or Daddy to be a "stranger" – even grandparents. Be patient with this phase. You are the centre of her universe, and she doesn't yet understand the concept of time, or know that when you leave her, you will definitely be coming back.

Your baby needs plenty of loving sympathy, as these fears seem very real to her.

● Loss of a comforter

Your baby may have become very attached to a security object, such as a dummy, a soft toy or even a scrap of cloth. It can cause great distress and crying if it gets lost or mislaid, most often in her cot during the night.

Make sure you have a spare one in case the precious original is lost for good, and always remember to take the comforter with you whenever you are out or staying away from home.

● Frustration

As your baby grows, she inevitably wants to try to do more, such as attempting to crawl before she's quite ready to or grab an interesting looking toy that's just out of her reach, and is likely to cry when she realizes that she can't manage to do everything – or have everything – that she wants! She needs lots of help and comfort from you to prevent this frustration becoming overwhelming for her.

● Bumps and bruises

Once on the move, babies can hurt themselves in lots of ways that don't happen to younger babies, and the

What are nightmares and night terrors?

Many children have nightmares, but a few may wake up crying from them. They happen in the lighter, dreaming (REM) phase of sleep, and older children can usually remember them in the morning. Reassure your baby and settle her back to sleep.

Night terrors are less common. They occur during deep sleep, and are not remembered on waking. They can be frightening for parents to witness. Your baby may be screaming, and thrashing around, but she will not be awake, so doesn't know what is happening. It is often better not to attempt to wake her up, but to try to gently soothe, perhaps whispering, "It's OK, I'm here. Don't be scared", and stroking gently.

If your baby's night terrors really worry you, try to spot a pattern. If they happen, for example, three hours after your baby goes to sleep, try to rouse her shortly before that time. Hopefully, you'll be able to settle her back to sleep again and intercept the event. Your baby will grow out them, without any harmful or long-term effects.

resulting bumps and knocks can lead to more tears. Plan ahead to childproof your home as your baby becomes more mobile. As well as protecting her from accidents, it can save frustration in the early years. Babies and toddlers do not have the ability to remember the word "No!" and repeating it can sometimes reinforce bad behaviour. With the freedom to explore safely, you will avoid having to repeat it to her until she is old enough to understand.

● **"Grizzling" and "fussing"**

This type of crying can be common in some older babies, while others may never do it. It can help to treat this as your baby's "conversation" and chat back to her, saying for example, "You're probably feeling bored going around this shop" or "You don't like sitting in that car seat, do you?" Anything interesting to create a distraction – for example, giving her a set of keys to jangle – will keep her amused for a while.

● **Night crying**

By around the age of three months, most babies can sleep for five-hour stretches at night, but one-third of babies still wake at one year, so there is wide variation, and a lot of babies will still be waking and crying in the night (see page 48).

ON THE MOVE
Whether she's rolling, crawling or already up on her feet, your older baby is likely to cry more from frustration or as a result of bumps as she struggles to perfect her skills.

WHERE IS SHE?
Peekaboo is more than just a game – it's teaching your baby "object permanence", that someone she loves is still there even though she can't see her.

Settling herself to sleep

You may have already started establishing ways to teach your baby to settle herself to sleep (see page 19). From four months, such routines become important both for daytime naps and at bedtime.

• At the age of four months, your baby will need two daytime naps of two to three hours each. By nine months, these will probably be reduced to one to two hours each. It's best to try to put her down for these naps while she's still awake and at roughly the same time each day.

• Continue keeping bedtimes peaceful. Set up a calm "winding down" period with a recognizable routine, such as a bath, song or bedtime story, so that your baby always knows that "sleep time" is coming up.

• Aim to put her down in her cot while she's drowsy but still awake, so that she learns how it feels to fall asleep on her own and develops her own self-soothing strategies. She's also less likely to wake in the night and cry, because her surroundings are familiar and she can go back to sleep by herself.

• Reconsider any comforting routines you have been using so far, such as giving her a dummy, or lying down with her or stroking her to settle her to sleep. From four months, your baby will expect these as part of her routine, and once firmly established, they will be hard to change.

New challenges

It's important to allow your baby plenty of time to adjust slowly to any changes to her routine, whether it's her first tastes of solid food or a new childcare arrangement. Despite her developing maturity, it is asking too much of your baby to expect her to happily accept major changes overnight without some protest.

You will avoid unnecessary tears if you are always sympathetic to your baby's fears. Give her plenty of cuddles and loving attention to help her deal with them. Many babies take a while to adjust to new situations, and your baby is likely to need patient understanding from you for some time to come.

Questions & Answers

My eight-month-old son had been sleeping through until about 6 am for some time – I thought that was it! But for the last week or two he's started waking and crying at least twice during the night. Why is this?

It is quite common for a baby who had begun to show signs of sleeping through the night to start waking and crying again at around eight to nine months. Babies this age might be more easily disturbed because they're more aware of their surroundings, and they may also find it harder to drop back to sleep without you to help them. They may have become very attached to a particular method of going to sleep, whether that involves sucking a dummy, holding a toy, or being cuddled by you, so they then need this again when they wake at night – even several times a night. Help him to develop better sleep habits (see right) and see if you can settle him back into a good night-time routine where he can fall back to sleep on his own.

Night waking

Up to about six months of age, your baby will probably wake during the night. She may still wake to be fed during the night, but beyond six months if she wakes it is more likely to be because she wants comfort or because something has disturbed her. Night waking can also be a sign of growth spurts – both physical and developmental.

Waking up in the dark and silence can make her puzzled and frightened, and if she is unable to settle herself back to sleep, she will start crying for you.

It's quite common from this age for babies who had been sleeping through for some time to start a phase of night waking again (see *Questions & Answers*, left).

We all stir from time to time during the night as we move between states of quiet and active (REM) sleep, but most of the time we're able simply to drift off to sleep again. Babies need to learn how to do this, and there are ways in which you can encourage your baby to develop good sleep habits.

● Resist going in to your baby at the first whimper. She may just be stirring and if you leave her a minute or two she may stop crying and settle on her own.

" Jack's cuddly blanket has a magical effect. He stops crying as soon as I hand it to him. "

NEIL is dad to eight-month-old Jack

- You may want to try methods to encourage better sleep (see below), which are taught by some health professionals to parents to help manage their babies' crying and sleeplessness. The aim is to help your baby settle herself to sleep at bedtime and if she wakes at night.
- Try to avoid lifting her from the cot when she wakes (see below) but, if you have to, keep the room dark, speak quietly or rock her soothingly. You are aiming to help her understand that night–time is for sleeping, not for playing.
- If she regularly wakes at night, there could be something disturbing her. Check that she's not too hot or too cold and that her room is not too light or too dark. Consider also

whether she's being woken by a noise – perhaps she can hear you stirring if she's still sleeping in your room.
- Try to keep reminding yourself that these night-waking episodes are a very short time in a child's

life. If you can deal patiently with your baby now, she will eventually feel secure in the knowledge that you or your partner will always come to her when you are needed, to answer calls of distress.

Encouraging better sleep

"Sleep training" can encourage your older baby (from six months) to settle on her own, safe in the knowledge that you are there but understanding that her waking will not be rewarded with a cuddle or a feed.

Allow at least a week for it to start taking effect, and you may need to be prepared for things to get worse before they start getting better. Share the checking routine with your partner, if possible, but you both need to be consistent in your approach. Only try this when you are sure that your baby is not ill, hungry or in any form of discomfort.

You can encourage your baby to sleep in the following way.
- Adopt a "checking" routine – start by waiting for five minutes when she wakes crying before going in to her.

When you leave the room, she will probably continue to cry but wait for a minute longer than last time before going to check her again.

- Each time you go in to check her, keep the room dark, speak softly to her, stroke her, but don't pick her up. Firmly say goodnight and leave the room. It's important to stay calm – you will probably have to do this several times before your baby falls asleep.

- For babies who need you with them to settle down to sleep, try a gradual retreat, or "fading". Again, this works over several nights and involves you staying in the room with your baby until she falls asleep, but each night moving further away from her cot. Eventually, you will be outside the room when she falls asleep.

How can I comfort my older baby?

There are so many ways you can comfort your older baby. Toys and games are now a ready source of amusement to share with her if she's crying for your attention, while diversions and distractions work well when tears of frustration are threatening. And, of course, there will still be times when only a loving cuddle will do.

New ways to comfort her

★ **Toys** Choosing toys that are suitable for her stage of development will entertain your baby best. This is not just to ensure that the toy is safe for her to use, but also to avoid frustration if it's beyond her capabilities. Once she can grasp, she'll love rattles or musical toys. When she sits up, stacking cups and shape sorters will be fun. As soon as she's mobile, she'll enjoy anything she can push or pull. And nearer her first birthday, she'll be ready for simple puzzles.

★ **Laughter** Using humour will often avoid tears. Singing a song, such as "This is the way we wash our hands", can amuse your baby when routine tasks need to be done.

CUDDLE UP
You're still your baby's best comforter. She doesn't want to be apart from you at the moment, and a hug from you can make everything better, helping her feel secure, loved, and allaying her fears.

★ **Action rhymes** Songs and rhymes with actions to learn together, such as "Humpty Dumpty", "Pat-a-cake" or "The wheels on the bus", can be energetic and great fun. Games that lead to a tickle and a hug, such as "This little piggy" and "Round and round the garden", will soon become familiar to her and have her giggling in anticipation of the ending.

★ **Distractions and diversions** If you see trouble brewing, quickly try to turn your baby's attention to a new toy, or something that may be happening outside: "Oh listen, I think I can hear Daddy coming" or "Can you see a cat in the garden?" If she's playing with something you'd rather she didn't have, offer her an interesting alternative rather than simply taking it away.

MAKE MUSIC TOGETHER
Musical instruments are not just for singing along to. Your baby will learn "cause and effect", that by banging, shaking or blowing she can make a sound happen. Even some pans and a wooden spoon will do – if you can bear the noise!

SHARE A BOOK
It's never too soon to introduce your baby to books. She'll enjoy hearing you tell the story again and again and will point out familiar objects in the colourful pictures. Books that have different textures for her to feel and lift-the-flap stories add to her interest.

" If things go wrong or Ben can't get his own way, he just drops to the floor, screaming. If he gets in a temper, I try to **distract him** with a favourite toy, or I might give him a **big cuddle** and talk to him. "

CAROLINE is mum to two-year-old Ben

7

Crying beyond babyhood

Between the ages of one and three, greater independence and mobility bring your child both new horizons and frustrations. He needs to be able to explore, but with the security of set boundaries, a predictable routine and your loving care. Soon he'll be ready to face the pre-school years, and all the challenges they will bring.

The toddler years

A toddler is a delightful little person, who can also present some fairly challenging behaviour. One minute, he wants to be treated like a baby; the next, to prove that he is really grown up and independent. Sensitive handling of your child at this stage can make a big difference to how much he is going to cry.

With his rapidly developing skills and mobility, your toddler is usually very determined to get his own way, yet has no real sense of the dangers or reasons why you might have to stop him doing appealing, but potentially harmful, things. He also has very little language to explain what he wants or, more importantly, how he feels.

It's a situation that could end up in a battle of wills, but try hard not to let that happen. Instead, keep one step ahead by ensuring that you have childproofed your home, moving all possible dangers out of reach and cutting down on potential frustrations for your child.

Positive discipline

Positive discipline is important for all children, but this is the perfect age to start. It involves giving positive attention, such as cuddles and praise, to behaviour you value and want to encourage – quiet play, sharing, being cheerful and kind – and trying to ignore the behaviours you don't want – manipulative crying and grizzling, tears and tempers.

This can be harder to do than it sounds. It is easy to fall into the trap of not noticing when children behave well, then jumping in to sort things out when they cry or make a fuss. Having said that, it is worth practising this positive approach to discipline so that it becomes second nature. Both you and your child will reap the benefits in the long term.

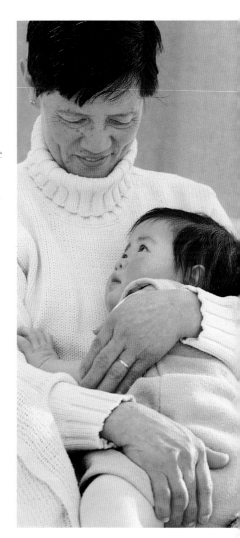

Questions & Answers

How can I break my three-year-old's habit of grizzling?
Sometimes your child may grizzle like this because she's hungry, tired or coming down with an illness, or she may simply be in a bad mood. Perhaps she feels she isn't getting enough of your attention, and resorts to this behaviour because she knows she will get a reaction from you, even a negative one. Try to make sure you praise her and give more positive attention when she is behaving nicely. When she grizzles, calmly refuse to respond to her requests until she stops and asks properly for what she wants.

Love and sympathy

Your newly mobile toddler will probably cry regularly over everyday bumps or scratches. In some cases, his crying won't be because of the pain – he may be really frightened by how easy and unexpected it is to be hurt. He may also be afraid of the sight of blood, however little there may be.

Loving sympathy is essential at this age. Give your child a reassuring cuddle and tell him you know that it hurts. Try saying, "Kiss it better", or use a "magic cream" when coming to his aid.

If you seem uncaring, your child is likely to cry even harder, and saying, "You're all right, it's hardly anything", can be confusing to him. Small children need you to accept their feelings and care about the things that are important to them.

Be aware also that your toddler is likely to pick up on any stresses, upsets or changes within the family, which could make him more tearful than usual. If it's appropriate, give him an explanation that he will understand to reassure him, together with plenty of cuddles and attention.

Monsters under the bed

Small children cannot always separate fact from fantasy. A shadow on the wall can easily look like a monster, the vacuum cleaner can seem as though it is threatening to swallow you up, the toilet flush may take you with it.

Many toddlers develop a fear of everyday tasks that didn't bother them as babies, such as hair washing or nail trimming. Try to let your toddler have some choices. It's easy to forget how frightening it is for children to feel as though they have no control over what happens to them.

Your pre-school child

As your child turns three, many of the causes of his crying as a toddler remain. He will resent not having his own way, and may continue to cry easily if he's frustrated or overtired.

He may still be scared by lots of things, and fears of monsters and

> *" I've found that sometimes a hug and a giggle at the right time can stop George's tears and tantrums. "*

ROBERT is grandfather of three-year-old George

Tantrums

Some children rarely have tantrums, according to parents, and others have them almost every day, or even more than once a day. Tantrums are not always inevitable – at least not the full-blown version – and the way you deal with this form of crying really does make a difference.

Children never start tantrums when no one is there – imagine your two-year-old popping into a room on his own to start a tantrum! Tantrums require an audience, and that audience is usually you.

● Tantrums might be more likely to happen when your child is tired, so make sure he has regular naps. Hunger may also be a contributing factor so, as well as his meals, give him healthy snacks throughout the day. Don't forget to take a snack with you when you are out and about.

● Frustration is a major cause of tantrums. He may feel overwhelmed by tasks he can't manage on his own, and inevitably there will be times when you have to stop your child doing something he wants to do. Tactfully, try to distract him so that tears don't turn into a tantrum.

● Take away his audience. If you are sure he can't hurt himself, calmly walk away into another room. But be sure to be there for him with a loving hug when it's all over.

● Probably nothing will work if your child is really out of control. Tantrums like this are very frightening for him, and it is essential for you to try to stay calm. Just be there to prevent your child hurting himself, or anyone else, and reassure him that you're there to help and comfort him.

ghosts become more likely because of his lively imagination. Be aware of the impact of frightening images he may see on television, or scary stories he might hear, if you don't want him becoming more fearful.

Out in the world

Your child may experience a whole set of new worries connected with playschool or nursery, such as making friends, or coping in strange situations. He may be overwhelmed by what to adults seem to be enjoyable activities, such as going to a party or on holiday, or during celebrations, such as birthdays.

Show your child you understand his reluctance, and support him until he feels ready to be grown up.

How can I comfort my toddler?

At this age your child is having to cope with many new challenges in her life. To help her cope and keep crying to a minimum, she needs the security of a routine, and plenty of love, hugs and support from you. Once you've eliminated the obvious causes of hunger, pain or tiredness, consider whether her crying is simply a way of seeking your attention. In which case, she will be instantly calmed if you join in a game with her favourite toy, do some drawing together or cuddle up with a book.

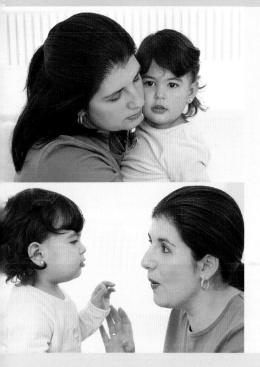

SPEND TIME TOGETHER
When your toddler's cries are telling you she needs your undivided attention, you could try a loving cuddle or try making her laugh by pulling funny faces with her.

READ A BOOK
Looking at picture books and reading stories is a perfect activity to do with your toddler – both as a way of giving her the positive attention she needs and as a distraction or to calm her if something has upset her and tears are looming.

There are many new tactics you can employ that will work well to ease your toddler's upsets.

★ **Talk with her** Now her understanding and speech are developing, you may be able to talk with her when tears threaten to take over. When telling her not to do something, instead of saying, "No!", use simple words to explain why you don't want her to do it – "Don't bite, it hurts Mummy."

★ **Adopt diversionary tactics** As far as possible, try to divert or distract your child as soon as you see trouble looming. "I think I hear the doorbell" takes her mind off, for example, the television controls. If you have no choice about stopping something, perhaps for safety reasons, be calm and firm and quickly distract her on to a new activity: "Look at this great book – let's read it."

★ **Accept that big boys do cry!** Avoid comments such as, "Don't be silly, you're too big now for crying." All children should be allowed, and even encouraged, to express their emotions without feeling they have to hold back the tears.

★ **Understand her feelings** Remember, your child will have sad and angry feelings, and her moods can alter in the same way an adult's can. Being a child means that she is still more likely to react to sad or upsetting situations by crying. Encourage her to talk and tell her you understand. Try to see the world from her point of view – think how she may be feeling when she cries. Be generous with your love and sympathy for genuine reasons.

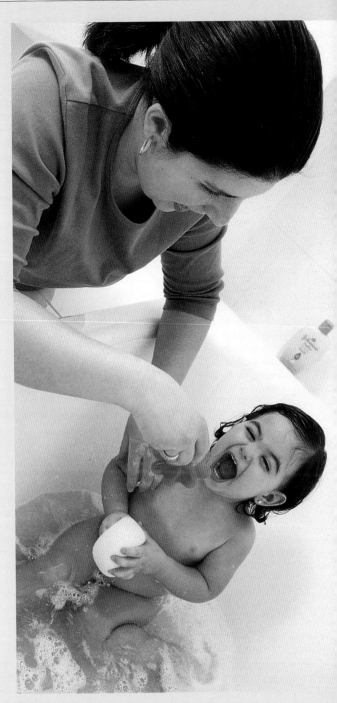

HAVE A BATH
An important part of her bedtime routine, having fun in the bath may persuade even the most sleep-resistant toddler to stop playing – and it will help her unwind, too.

" When Ryan was a baby, I took him to the doctor because I couldn't stop him crying one day. Luckily, there was **nothing wrong**, and his crying stopped when we got home. I could **relax** once I knew he was well. "

JENNY is mum to three-year-old Ryan

8

Seeking medical advice

It is natural to feel anxious about your baby's health and interpret persistent crying as a sign that she's ill. The chances are that your baby is fine and her crying is normal, but it is important to be alert to any worrying signs. Doctors will always take your concerns seriously so do not hesitate to seek advice, if only to put your mind at rest.

Help for your baby

Much research has shown that illness is a cause for crying in only a very small percentage of cases. Nevertheless, it is worth consulting your doctor, who can check that there are no underlying medical conditions or health problems, and reassure you that your baby is well.

You may think that crying is something you don't want to bother your doctor about, or you may even fear that you will be judged as a failure in some way if you admit that there are times when you find it hard to cope, but this is never the case.

Good advice

Healthcare professionals always view asking for help positively – you have had the courage to admit that looking after a baby is not always plain sailing. Every parent feels this, at least sometimes – even those who are experienced.

Even when excessive crying is not caused by illness, doctors usually have the experience of seeing many babies, and can offer you advice on managing your baby's crying that may have worked for other parents, or reassure you that you are certainly not alone.

Sometimes, you may hear conflicting advice from more than one source and this can be confusing, especially if you are a new parent. However, it's important to remember that there are not always clear-cut right and wrong answers about crying. What might have worked for other babies may have little benefit with yours.

You are the expert on your baby, and you can choose any advice that works for you and reject any that doesn't.

Checklist

Don't delay getting medical help if crying is accompanied by any of these signs:

- sudden unusual screaming, or a frantic cry – often a sign of pain
- crying that gets worse when you pick your baby up
- a lack of interest in feeding
- diarrhoea and/or vomiting
- an unusual rash that doesn't fade when pressed with the side of a glass
- not making eye contact or being unusually subdued
- a whimpering cry with fever – over 38°C (100.4°F) – or unusual lethargy
- a very swollen abdomen, or laboured or rapid breathing
- pulling at an ear, with fever or inconsolable crying.

Expert tips

Help your baby or child feel comfortable when she's ill.

• If your baby has a fever, take her temperature and consult your doctor if it is over 38°C (100.4°F). Give liquid paracetamol suitable for children according to your doctor's instructions.

• To make her feel more comfortable, and to try to reduce the fever, keep her room cool and dress her in lightweight cotton clothing.

• Give her plenty of fluids to drink, to avoid dehydration.

• Keep an eye on your baby, even when she's asleep. Put her down where you can see her.

The crying paradox

In one way, nature seems to have slipped up. Crying is obviously meant to elicit the care needed for survival, ensuring loving interaction and adequate nutrition from parents. Yet, when it goes on and on, it can become "aversive". Studies have shown that some parents feel angry and less sympathetic towards a baby who cries excessively. If you are experiencing this, you will be feeling vulnerable, and you need help and support now. Don't feel guilty – no one has infinite patience. Recognizing that you need help is a positive step, so consult your doctor, or call Cry-sis (see page 62).

Information to share

It will help you, and your doctor, to keep a diary of your baby's crying for a week or two. Armed with this information, your doctor will be better able to understand your concerns, and provide a plan of care that is more likely to help both you and your baby. Your diary should make note of:

• the average number of hours your baby cries per day

• the number of days a week that her crying is a problem

• the intensity of the crying

• the constancy of the crying

• the pattern of the crying, whether it happens at a particular time of day or at a certain point in your baby's routine, such as after she has been fed

• anything that seems to make the crying better or worse.

Minor conditions

There are a number of minor conditions that may cause your baby to cry and, again, your doctor, health visitor or pharmacist will be able to advise you on the best course of action to take to help her.

• **Colds and coughs** While colds are not usually serious, a blocked nose may cause your baby to cry from frustration when feeding as she won't be able to breathe properly.

KEEPING A CRYING DIARY
A diary is a useful record for your doctor, as well as a way of reassuring you that your baby's crying may not be as persistent as it seems!

Also, stuffiness and an irritating cough may keep her awake at night, making her overtired, and leading to crying. Ask your pharmacist to recommend an over-the-counter treatment suitable for your baby or child to use.

• **Nappy rash** Feeling sore means that urine may sting and cause your baby to cry every time she wets her nappy. Change her nappy frequently, letting the air get to her skin, and use a barrier cream to protect her.

• **Thrush** Oral thrush is a fungal infection that can make feeding painful. Look for white patches inside her mouth, which will not come off if you gently wipe them with a clean handkerchief. Your doctor may prescribe medication.

● **Teething** Once your baby starts cutting her teeth, she may experience some discomfort until the tooth breaks through her gum (see page 44).

● **Urinary tract infection** This can be hard for parents to spot in babies, although there may be a fever as well as more crying than usual. An older child may pass urine more frequently, and the urine may be cloudy or smelly. Your doctor will test your child's urine and prescribe antibiotics.

Complementary therapies

Complementary therapies are sometimes used by parents looking for ways of soothing their babies' crying. Massage is used to boost a baby's wellbeing and promote relaxation and bonding (see pages 22–23), while homeopathy can help with digestive problems.

Cranial osteopathy is used to improve persistent crying and to calm restless babies. It is based on the theory that cranial faults can develop when the bones of a baby's skull are compressed during birth. Very gentle manipulation is used to move them into the correct position.

Before visiting any complementary practitioner, ensure that he or she is registered and specializes in working with babies and children.

Questions & Answers

Whenever my baby cries more than usual, I always fret that he may be ill. My biggest fear is meningitis. How will I know?
This is a rare and extremely serious illness, but babies can recover with antibiotics if it is caught early. So if you ever suspect it, **take your baby to hospital immediately**. There are viral and bacterial types, and signs to look out for are a high-pitched, moaning cry, a very high temperature and your baby appearing sleepy or refusing to eat. One type, meningococcal meningitis, produces a red or purplish rash that doesn't fade when pressed with the side of a clear glass or your finger. Other types do not produce a rash, so never wait for this sign – seek medical help **as soon as possible**. There are vaccinations for meningitis C and haemophilus influenzae type b (Hib).

Useful contacts

Action for Sick Children
c/o The National Children's Bureau,
8 Wakley Street, London EC1V 7QE
Tel: 020 7843 6444
www.actionforsickchildren.org
Joins parents and professionals in
promoting high quality healthcare
for children in hospital and at home.

**Association for
Post-Natal Illness**
145 Dawes Road, London SW6 7EB
Tel: 020 7386 0868
www.apni.org
Advises, supports and provides
information on postnatal depression.

**Association of Breastfeeding
Mothers (ABM)**
Helpline (24-hours): 020 7813 1481
http://home.clara.net/abm
Gives mother-to-mother
breastfeeding support and
up-to-date breastfeeding information.

CRY-SIS
BM CRY-SIS, London WC1N 3XX
Helpline: 020 7404 5011
www.cry-sis.org.uk
Provides emotional support
and practical advice for parents
dealing with a baby's crying and
sleep problems.

Gingerbread
7 Sovereign Close, Sovereign Court,
London E1W 3HW
Helpline: 0800 018 4318
Office: 020 7488 9300
www.gingerbread.org.uk
Provides support and practical
help for lone-parent families.

Home-Start
2 Salisbury Road, Leicester LE1 5QR
Helpline: 0800 068 6368
Office: 0116 233 9955
www.home-start.org.uk
Provides training, information and
support to existing and potential
Home-Start schemes, which offer
support, friendship and practical help
to families with children under five.

La Leche League (GB)
PO Box 29, West Bridgford,
Nottingham NG2 7NP
Helpline (24 hours): 0845 120 2918
www.laleche.org.uk
Offers help and information to
mothers wishing to breastfeed.

**MAMA
(Meet-A-Mum Association)**
376 Bideford Green, Linslade,
Leighton Buzzard LU7 2TY
Tel: 01525 217064
www.mama.org.uk
Aims to help mothers who feel
depressed and isolated when their
babies are born, through the setting
up of local groups of mothers to talk
about their experiences.

National Childbirth Trust (NCT)
Alexandra House, Oldham Terrace,
London W3 6NH
Tel: 0870 444 8707
NCT Breastfeeding helpline:
0870 444 8708
www.nctpregnancyandbabycare.com
Provides support for pregnancy,
birth and early parenthood, and
gives information to enable parents
to make informed choices.

**NSPCC (National Society
for the Prevention of
Cruelty to Children)**
42 Curtain Road, London EC2A 3NH
Free confidential helpline:
0808 800 5000
Textphone: 0800 056 0566
www.nspcc.org.uk
UK's leading charity specializing
in child protection and the
prevention of cruelty to children.

**Osteopathic Centre
for Children**
109 Harley Street, London
W1 1DG
Tel: 020 7486 6160
www.occ.uk.com
Specializes in the treatment of
babies and children, and aims to
raise awareness of the benefits
of paediatric osteopathy.

Parentline Plus
Unit 520, Highgate Studios,
53-79 Highgate Road, London
NW5 1TL
Helpline: 0808 800 2222
www.parentlineplus.org.uk
Offers support and up-to-date
information to anyone parenting
a child.

**TAMBA (Twins and Multiple
Births Association)**
2 The Willows, Gardner Road,
Guildford GU1 4PG
Twinline: 0800 138 0509
www.tamba.org.uk
Encourages and offers support
to families and carers of twins,
triplets or more.